Crack!

Author:

Fiona Macdonald studied history at
Cambridge University and at the University of
East Anglia, both in England. She has taught in
schools and universities and is the author of
numerous books for children on historical topics.

Artist:

David Antram was born in Brighton, England,
in 1958. He studied at Eastbourne College of Art
and then worked in advertising for 15 years before
becoming a full-time artist. He has illustrated
many children's nonfiction books.

Series creator:

David Salariya was born in Dundee, Scotland.
He has illustrated a wide range of books and has
created and designed many new series for
publishers in the UK and overseas. David
established The Salariya Book Company in 1989.
He lives in Brighton with his wife, illustrator
Shirley Willis, and their son, Jonathan.

Editor: Stephen Haynes

Editorial Assistant: Mark Williams

PAPER FROM
SUSTAINABLE
FORESTS

© The Salariya Book Company Ltd MMX

Published in Great Britain in 2010 by
The Salariya Book Company Ltd
25 Marlborough Place, Brighton BN1 1UB

ISBN-13: 978-0-531-20504-4 (lib. bdg.)   978-0-531-13784-0 (pbk.)
ISBN-10: 0-531-20504-5 (lib. bdg.)   0-531-13784-8 (pbk.)

All rights reserved.
Published in 2010 in the United States
by Franklin Watts
An imprint of Scholastic Inc.
Published simultaneously in Canada.

A CIP catalog record for this book is available
from the Library of Congress.

Printed and bound in China.
Printed on paper from sustainable sources.
1 2 3 4 5 6 7 8 9 10 R 19 18 17 16 15 14 13 12 11 10

You Wouldn't Want to Work on a Medieval Cathedral!

Written by
Fiona Macdonald

Illustrated by
David Antram

Created and designed by
David Salariya

A Difficult Job That Never Ends

Franklin Watts®
An Imprint of Scholastic Inc.
NEW YORK • TORONTO • LONDON • AUCKLAND • SYDNEY
MEXICO CITY • NEW DELHI • HONG KONG
DANBURY, CONNECTICUT

Contents

Introduction

Hello there! Welcome to Canterbury, an ancient city that's home to England's most important cathedral. Travelers come from far and wide to visit.

Meet my grandson. Come over here, lad, and say hello! He'll be twelve soon—born around 1370, if my memory's right. Soon it will be time for him to start work.

Have you chosen a career yet, laddie? Eh? Eh? You want to be a builder, like your father and like me, your old grandpa? Well, it's a good job, the pay's not bad, and you could work with us, of course. But what's that you say? You want to be an expert, the very best?

You want to be a cathedral builder?

5

A Grand Tradition

These days, cathedrals are real eye-catchers. They're designed in the latest, daring styles and built with the very best materials. And, of course, they're always being made bigger and more beautiful.

What are cathedrals for? Why, surely you know that! They're huge, elegant churches, where people worship God and think about heaven. And they're also headquarters for busy bishops.

Cathedral-building would be a thrilling job, but, believe me, it's not easy. You'd need years of training and hard work, as well as natural talent. Do you think you're ready for that challenge?

Durham Cathedral, Durham, England c. 1093–1133

Canterbury

YOU LIVE HERE

Notre Dame de Paris, France c. 1163–1250

Catedral de Santiago de Compostela, Galicia, Spain c. 1075–1211

What Is a Cathedral?

HOLY THRONE. The word *cathedral* comes from *cathedra*, the Latin (and Greek) name for a bishop's throne.

HOUSE OF GOD. To Christians, cathedrals are filled with God's Holy Spirit. They are beautiful, holy places to say prayers.

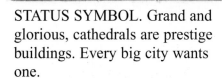

STATUS SYMBOL. Grand and glorious, cathedrals are prestige buildings. Every big city wants one.

Cathedrals are the finest buildings in Europe, magnificently decorated with carvings, stained glass, glittering jewels, and sculptures. They don't all look the same; each is a unique work of art. Here are just a few of the most famous.

Speyer, Germany
c. 1030–1106

St. Mark's, Venice, Italy
c. 829–1071

Duomo, Pisa, Italy
c. 1063–1272

Handy Hint

Build with the best materials! Most people live in fragile timber buildings that don't last long. But cathedrals are made of stone, and built to last!

BAND OF BROTHERS. Some cathedrals also have a monastery attached. Brotherhoods of monks live there, devoting their lives to God. They take part in cathedral prayers and sing in cathedral choirs.

ROYAL CONNECTIONS. Kings are crowned in cathedrals. They hope that God will help them rule, and protect them.

The Story So Far

BY THE 14th CENTURY, Canterbury Cathedral already has a history that stretches back hundreds of years.

1. c. 597–602. First cathedral is built by Augustine using the remains of an old Roman church. It is later rebuilt twice. Burned down by Vikings in 1011, it is rebuilt a third time by 1038.

2. c. 1067–1077. Cathedral is again destroyed by fire; it's replaced by a new-style building planned by Archbishop Lanfranc from France.

3. c. 1098–1130. Archbishop Anselm initiates the addition of buildings decorated in Italian, Greek, and Muslim styles, and a crypt.

Long-Term Project

Tell me, my lad, how big is our house? Yes, four rooms, an attic, and a workshop. And we are well off; most people nowadays live in cottages with one or two rooms.

Now, compare those cottages with Canterbury Cathedral over there. It's gigantic! It has pillars and arches, porches and niches, vast windows, steep roofs—and much more! Just think how complicated it was to design each part—and how long it took to construct them all! Cathedral-building takes centuries. It's a very slow process, aiming for perfection.

4. c. 1174–1184. Another fire, and more rebuilding. A second crypt is added, as well as new chapels. One houses the shrine of St. Thomas Becket (see page 22).

5. c. 1377–1410. The nave (main hall) of the cathedral will be replaced by a splendid new one, with wonderful arches and carvings and a vaulted roof (see page 19).

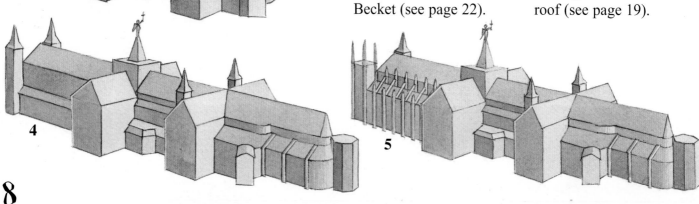

Angel Steeple

Canterbury Cathedral is 525 feet (160 m) long and 154 feet (47 m) wide. The tip of its Angel Steeple is 236 feet (72 m) high.

Handy Hint

Make friends with the rich and famous! New buildings at Canterbury are being paid for by a wealthy well-wisher.

You won't see another one like it anywhere!

Are You a Good Team Player?

Meet the Team

DEVISER. Designs each new section of the cathedral building and marks out full-size patterns on the floor for masons and carvers to follow.

It takes hundreds of people, all with different skills, to create a cathedral. If you want to share in their grand project, you must be able to cooperate with them. Learn to give and take, and be cheerful and polite. If you help others, they'll help you! But if you're rude or lazy, expect big trouble.

Cathedral builders are respected for the quality of their work. Their skills and knowledge are essential. Which building craft will you choose to learn? None of them are easy!

Ow!

WOODCARVER (below). Uses razor-sharp tools to decorate doors, seats, screens, and pulpits with wonderful shapes and patterns.

Aaargh!

QUARRYMAN. Hacks huge hunks of rock from cliffs and hammers them into rough slabs for the masons.

WOODWORKERS. Sawyers saw tall tree trunks into neat planks. Joiners make doors and window frames. Skilled carpenters build rafters and scaffolding.

Wheeze!

MASON (left). Some masons shape rough-cut stone into precise building blocks. Others decorate blocks with carvings. It's a dusty job!

How's that window going to fit into this frame?

Quit being rude, or I'll report you to the guild!

Handy Hint

Join a craftsman's guild. There's one for each trade. In most cities, you can't get a skilled job unless you're a guild member.

Do You Have the Muscle Power?

In the 14th century, there are no power tools or engines. You must construct buildings by hand, using simple technology and an enormous amount of muscle power. Cathedral builders must be tough, hard-working, and strong!

ROOFER (left). Covers wooden roofs with sheets of lead (or with tiles made of stone) to keep out rain and snow.

GLAZIER (below). Creates glorious windows using pieces of stained glass that are held in place by lead borders.

BELL-MAKER. Makes beautiful-sounding church bells by pouring molten bronze into molds formed in the ground.

He might have what it takes...

Learning on the Job

You say you'd like to be a stonemason? That's a good idea, but whatever skill you decide to learn, you'll need a master to teach you. For seven years, you must promise to study, work hard, and obey him. You'll live in his house as an apprentice—part student, part servant. You'll run errands, watch your master work, and ask lots of questions. The master will teach you all you need to know, from roughly shaping stone to carving delicate details. When the apprenticeship ends, you'll be older and wiser, and you'll graduate as a journeyman. Then you can work for anyone you choose, and you'll be paid by the day.

Now you've done it!

Crack!

YOUR MASTER pays a scribe to write an indenture—a legal contract that spells out his promise to train you in return for your labor. The indenture is torn in two—your master keeps one half, your parents the other. The jagged edges can be lined up to prove that the contract is genuine.

Handy Hint

Be good to your guild brothers. They'll teach you the tricks of the trade and support you in hard times.

Do you have any idea how much that stone costs?

sniff

SAY GOOD-BYE to your family! Now you must rely on yourself to survive. Quick thinking and a willingness to learn will help you.

WORRIED AND CONFUSED in your new surroundings? Be brave! You'll soon get used to your master's busy household.

chip chip chip

EXHAUSTED by days in the workshop? Your muscles will soon become stronger and you'll learn many clever techniques.

13

Have Mallet, Will Travel

Now, imagine that you're a journeyman. You're almost 20 years old, with no home, no food, no money—and no master to guide you. You have training, but no experience.

Listen to an old man's advice, my lad! You need to find work—hard, boring work, and plenty of it. Take every building job you can. Build up your knowledge, your savings, and your strength. Then, perhaps, a team of cathedral builders might be willing to employ you.

SAY GOOD-BYE to your master. He's taught you all he can. Now you must fend for yourself.

Summer sun

Spring showers

Way-hey!

AWAKENED BY NOISY PARTYGOERS at a busy roadside inn? Pull the blankets over your ears and try to block out the noise!

Kyrie eleison!
(Lord, have mercy!)

Life on the Road

LOOKING FOR LODGINGS at the local monastery? Remember, monks get up at midnight to chant their first prayers of the morning!

Fall windstorms

AS A JOURNEYMAN, you may work on a project for days, weeks, or years, until your task is completed. But then you'll need to find new work—and quickly! Be prepared to walk miles between building sites—and to face dangers along the way.

Woooooo...

CROUCHED ON A CHURCH PORCH? Then you'll need strong nerves. Bats, owls, and other creatures of the night have a habit of lurking there.

Cockadoodle doo!

Snort!

Winter snows

SEEKING SHELTER with peasants? They bring their livestock indoors at night—and some creatures can get *far* too close for comfort!

BEDDED DOWN IN A BARN? Then beware of the bull and other big animals sleeping there. They may not welcome sharing their space with strangers!

15

Practice Makes Perfect

Think ahead ten more years. You've survived life as a traveling journeyman. It's been tough, but you've learned a lot from your fellow workers and from the sights you've seen on your travels. Your next step will be to apply for a job helping to improve Canterbury Cathedral.

But what's this splendid statue you've been working on secretly? It's your test piece! I hope the masons' jury likes it—if they do, you'll qualify as a master mason. You'll win prestige, more money, and respect from your friends and neighbors. Even more importantly, you'll get the chance to create all kinds of stonework for the cathedral.

Will You Pass the Test?

A JURY of expert stonemasons will examine your test sculpture. Will they find fault and reject it—or praise it as your masterpiece?

Of course, it's a bit modern for my taste.

Nice work, though.

GARGOYLES. These funny, scary faces (1) hide pipes that carry rainwater away from the walls and roofs.

BUTTRESSES (2) prevent high walls from leaning outward.

STATUES of favorite saints (3) remind worshippers of heaven.

ARCHES (4) hold up roofs and floors. Until around 1150, arches were made wide and rounded. Now, in the 1380s, they are narrow and pointed.

PILLARS support the arches. Most have decorated capitals at the top (5). Pillars may be carved to look like a cluster of narrow columns (6). Sometimes they are multicolored.

CARVED FRIEZES decorate the walls (7).

STONE SLABS OR TILES cover the floor (8). There may also be a maze—a symbol of the soul's search for God.

Grand Designs

What's next? Why not apply to help a famous master mason design a new chapel? If you get that job, you really will have reached the top of your profession!*

It's a job that comes with big responsibilities. Design mistakes can lead to terrible disasters. Have you heard of Ely Cathedral? In 1322, a badly designed stone tower crashed through its roof to the floor!

With luck, the master mason will show you how to create exciting new designs. You'll study old buildings, make lots of measurements, and draw sketches. Some masons base their designs on mysterious mathematical calculations, which they say contain holy secrets!

* In the 14th century, the job of architect has not yet been invented.

Dual Purpose

Flying buttress

Nave wall

MANY CATHEDRAL FEATURES are designed with a double purpose: to be useful *and* to look good. Graceful "flying buttresses" support walls without blocking the light from the windows.

KEEP A SKETCHBOOK, as French artist Villard de Honnecourt did in the 13th century.

BE BOLD! EXPERIMENT! Make trial drawings of your own building plans on a floor covered with wet plaster.

SLIM PINNACLES add weight to stonework to make it more stable.

Pinnacle

Top of buttress

RIB VAULTING spreads the weight of the ceiling, carrying weight down to the ground.

Vault

Ribs

Pillars

We'll have to get the builders in again.

Ely Cathedral, 1322: The central tower gives way, after standing for 200 years. It's lucky that no one is killed.

Handy Hint

Make good foundations, or your building will never stand straight. Look at the famous Leaning Tower at Pisa Cathedral in Italy. It's built on soft sand and clay!

Health and Safety

After you become a master mason, it'll be your job to plan and manage all the different stages of construction. You must organize your masons: some will "set out" (make templates for others to copy); less-skilled masons will saw and "bank" (rough-cut) blocks into shape; and expert carver-masons will create the finished stonework. You must also give orders to the other craftsmen on site—and keep tight control of the budget!

At times, you'll get tired and stressed, but always keep your own safety in mind. Remember what happened to master mason William of Sens, right here in Canterbury. He climbed 50 feet (15 m) up to examine some stonework—and fell off the scaffolding!

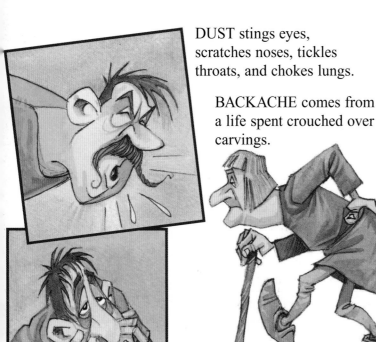

DUST stings eyes, scratches noses, tickles throats, and chokes lungs.

CARRYING HEAVY LOADS wears out a person's joints.

BACKACHE comes from a life spent crouched over carvings.

Creak

POISONOUS LEAD makes roofers and glaziers very, very sick.

GLASS FURNACES glow red-hot. They burn and blister skin.

Forced Retirement

At first, William of Sens tried to keep working from his sickbed. But he was too ill, and he soon left Canterbury for France, his homeland. He died there in 1180, a year after his accident. His designs were completed by a new master mason, William the Englishman, in 1184.

Handy Hint

Carry an amber amulet (charm). According to Arab doctors—some of the best in the 14th century—it will prevent joint pain.

Where'd he go?

Aaaaargh!

Could You Stand Up to an Abbot?

Are you courteous, tactful, smooth-talking, clear-headed, calm—and strong-minded? You'll need all of these qualities when you talk to the people who pay for cathedral construction. They range from kings, queens, and local landowners to senior priests and abbots (heads of monasteries). Most will have traveled to France and other countries and seen fascinating buildings there. They may want you to copy them.

These rich and powerful people are used to getting their own way. They don't like to be contradicted! But you must persuade them that your plan is the best.

Outspoken Bishops

CHURCHMEN often have strong views. In 1170, Canterbury's own archbishop, Thomas Becket, was murdered in the cathedral by royal soldiers after a conflict with King Henry II. Now Becket's buried close to where he died, in a beautiful new chapel.

Local Worthies

LEADING LOCALS—lords and ladies, mayors and merchants (left)—are very proud of "their" cathedral. They are always willing to give money, but they like to be consulted in return. Be sensitive to their feelings!

Handy Hint

Be trustworthy. William the Englishman (see page 21) got the job because he was "acute [clever] and honest."

There he goes again…

It's got to be better than anything the French have got.

Clever Machines

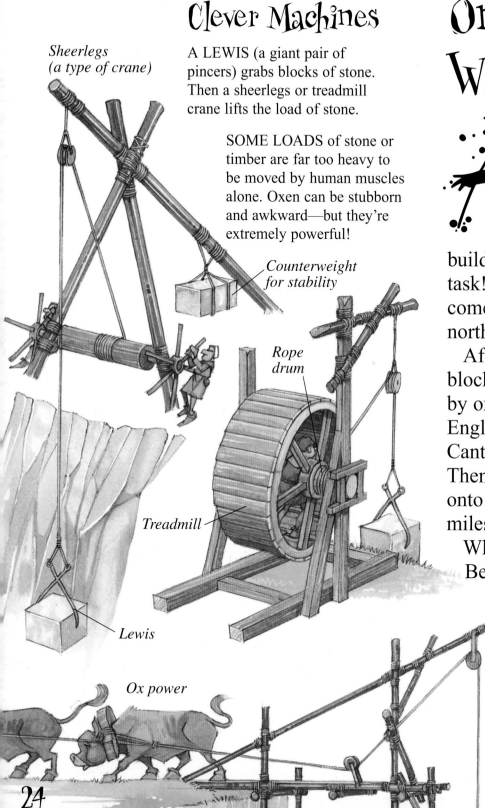

Sheerlegs (a type of crane)

A LEWIS (a giant pair of pincers) grabs blocks of stone. Then a sheerlegs or treadmill crane lifts the load of stone.

SOME LOADS of stone or timber are far too heavy to be moved by human muscles alone. Oxen can be stubborn and awkward—but they're extremely powerful!

Counterweight for stability

Rope drum

Treadmill

Lewis

Ox power

Only the Best Will Do

As master mason, it's also your job to find building stone for the cathedral and have it transported to the building site. That's no easy task! The stone for Canterbury comes all the way from Caen in northern France.

After the stone is chopped into blocks at the quarry, it's taken by oxcart to the coast, sailed to England on ships, and ferried to Canterbury by river barges. Then the stone is loaded back onto oxcarts for the last few miles of its journey.

Why go to all that trouble? Because Caen stone is some of the best in the world. It's limestone, with a smooth, fine texture and a lovely pale cream color. It can be cut and carved in any direction without splitting or cracking.

Pestered by Pilgrims

Like all 14th-century Christians, you honor saints and believe that their prayers will help you get to heaven. Canterbury Cathedral houses the relics (remains) of famous local saint Thomas Becket. A gold, jeweled casket in the Trinity Chapel holds his body; the Corona (a circular chapel) contains part of his skull.

Every year, thousands of pilgrims flock to Canterbury to see the relics. Their gifts of money help pay for building work—but these visitors cause problems! They need food, drink, lodgings, and entertainment. And all too often, they get rowdy.

Who do you think you are—the Archbishop of Canterbury?

It should be a best seller!

Canterbury Tales

MANY PILGRIMS treat their journey as an enjoyable vacation. They ride fine horses, stay in cozy inns, and amuse each other with funny stories. Around this time, England's top poet, Geoffrey Chaucer, is writing a collection of such stories.

In 1370, Archbishop Sudbury had to run for his life when angry pilgrims came after him. He had scolded them for bad behavior.

Handy Hint

Fire has destroyed many churches and cathedrals—including Canterbury. So watch out for the candles that pilgrims light when they pray.

I shall not be moved.

I wonder how fast he can run in those robes.

Royal Resting Place

KINGS AND PRINCES pay good money to be buried in the cathedral. Best known is Edward, the "Black Prince," son of King Edward III. When this famous warrior died in 1376, Henry Yevele (see page 17) designed a magnificent gold and bronze tomb for him.

He never wore shoes like that, you know. Not while I knew him.

Why was Edward called the Black Prince? Some say that it's because he wore black armor or carried a black shield, but nobody knows for sure.

Building for the Future

Well! You've seen what the future might hold if you choose to be a cathedral builder: long years of study, tough tests of skill, lots of hard work, and heavy responsibilities. Are you still sure that it's the right career for you? If so, good luck! But, before you start, there's one other problem to consider.

Could you really devote your life to work that you'll never see completed? Not sure? Then think about this: if you could travel hundreds of years into the future, you'd find that most of Europe's great cathedrals are still standing, proud and beautiful—and millions of people still worship in and visit them.

After You're Gone...

I'd make it taller.

A NEW MASTER MASON will take over. Will he honor your plans and your vision—or have his own ideas?

CENTURIES of wind, rain, frost, and snow will shatter the strongest stone. In the 21st century, Canterbury Cathedral will urgently need work to save it from falling down!

WARTIME TARGET. In the 17th century, the English Parliament's army will smash stained glass at Canterbury.* During World War II, Canterbury's towers will be bombed.

28   ** These soldiers were very strict Christians who believed it was sinful to admire beautiful images.*

THE CATHEDRAL TODAY contains work from every period from the 11th century to the 19th century.

Handy Hint

Sign your work. Some masons do so by hiding pictures of themselves among the carvings.

...and their amazing work is still standing today!

Glossary

Apprentice A young person who learns a trade by working for a master, usually without pay.

Arch A curved structure that spans an opening and serves as a support. An arch is much stronger than a flat-topped opening.

Archbishop A top-ranking bishop with authority over other bishops.

Bishop A senior churchman with authority over ordinary priests.

Budget The amount of money available to spend on a project.

Buttress A strong, heavy prop built against the side of a wall to prevent the wall from leaning.

Capital A block at the top of a pillar, carved in a decorative shape.

Cathedral A church that is the headquarters of a bishop.

Chapel A place of worship within a church or other building.

Cloister A courtyard with a covered walkway around the edge.

Crypt An underground cellar or basement.

Flying buttress A buttress that is built some distance away from a wall and connected to the wall by half-arches.

Foundation The lowest part of a building, which supports the whole building by spreading its weight into the earth.

Frieze A band of carved decoration along the surface of a wall.

Guild An organization of workers in a particular profession. A guild helps its members and prevents non-members from working in the profession.

Journeyman A worker who has finished his apprenticeship but has not yet qualified as a master. He is paid by the day—the name comes from the French word *journée*, which means "a day" or "a day's work."

Mason A worker who builds in stone.

Master A worker who has passed a test to prove that he is skilled in his trade. He is allowed to employ other workers and to train apprentices.

Master mason A mason who has qualified as a master; also, the head mason on a building project.

Masterpiece A test piece made by a worker as part of the examination to become a master mason.

Molten Melted by heating to a very high temperature.

Monastery The home of a community of monks.

Niche A shallow opening in a wall, usually meant to hold a statue.

Pilgrim A person who travels to visit holy places and relics.

Pillar A tall, narrow support for a ceiling or a wall.

Pinnacle A tall, narrow ornament, placed on top of a buttress to stabilize it.

Pulpit The platform that a priest stands on while leading a worship service.

Rafter A sloping piece of wood that is part of the structure of a roof.

Relic A part of a saint's body or an article that belonged to a saint.

Rib A narrow band of stone that helps to strengthen a vault.

Scribe In the Middle Ages, a person who wrote or copied official documents.

Shrine In some Christian religions, a place that holds relics of a saint.

Template A pattern of wood or metal used as a guide to cut stone into a certain shape.

Vault A roof with an arched shape, which is much stronger than a flat or sloping roof.

Index